Skylandia

farm poetry from Maine

Skylandia: Farm Poetry From Maine
Copyright © 2015 by Rivera Sun

All rights reserved. Printed in the United States of America. No part of this book may be used or reproduced in any manner whatsoever without written permission except in the case of brief quotations embodied in critical articles and reviews. For information address:

Rising Sun Press Works
P.O. Box 1751, El Prado, NM 87529
www.riverasun.com

Library of Congress Control Number
2015947465

ISBN 978-0-9966391-8-7
Sun, Rivera 1982-
Skylandia: Farm Poetry From Maine

Cover photos by Rivera Sun
Portrait Photo by Steve DiBartolomeo

Dedicated to the Farm

Other Works
by Rivera Sun

Novels, Books & Poetry
Billionaire Buddha
The Dandelion Insurrection
Steam Drills, Treadmills, and Shooting Stars
Freedom Stories: volume one
The Imagine-a-nation of Lala Child

Theatrical Plays & Presentations
Jimmy/Joan
Stone Soup
The Imagine-a-nation of Lala Child
The Education of Lala Girl
The Emancipation of Lala

RISING SUN
PRESS WORKS

Skylandia

farm poetry from Maine

by

Rivera Sun

Table of Contents

Skylandia	1
Tangle of Limbs	2
Up North	3
In the Kingdom	4
Roadside Farm Stands	6
Farmhouse	8
Walking the Edge	10
Down on My Knees in Devotion	12
Bouquets of Mother	14
Selling Poetry, Not the Farm	16
Raspberry Queen	20
The Other Maine	23
Efficiency	25
Mosquitos on Wall St.	27
Open for Business	29
Alive	32
North Slope Orchard	38
Born and Raised in California	39
Woods	42
Potato Barn	43
Onward!	44
Hard Rocks and Potatoes	46
Snow Carrots	47
Awake	49
Autumn Crisp	50
Four O'clock Dark	51
Breathless	52
Dead of Winter	53
Farm Marrow	54
North Country Mornings	55
Baptism	57

Agricultural Old	58
Good Earth	59
Afternoon Patina	60
Days of Downpour	61
Candlelight & Rain	62
Compost Psalm	63
Thunderstorm Joy	64
Daybreak Poem	66
The World Spoke Poetry	67
Skinny Onions	69
Transplant	71
Novelist Grown	72
Library Books	73
Family	76
If it is Good . . .	77
Hot Tar Fiddler on the Roof	79
Memory Footage	81
Summer of Canning Tomatoes	83
Flatbed Truck	86
Growing Change	89
Hermit Crab Shell	93
Thirty-three	94
Been Gone Long	95

Skylandia

farm poetry from Maine

Skylandia

Skylandia
a place where
clouds sail
over pine forests
and sweep down
deep, cold lakes
over fields of wild grasses.

A place located
at the crossroads
of reality and myth
on a map that requires
faith to unfold
where belief unlocks
a farmhouse that has no keys
and the taste of raspberries
tumbles down hillsides.

Tangle of Limbs

I grew up
in a tangle of limbs
four siblings' worth
of skinned knees
and close shaves
childhood scrapes
like a pack of puppies
mischief amplified by ten
there was nothing
we couldn't get into
out of
or in trouble for
that tangle of limbs
and me.

Up North

Up north,
stars brush the tips
of outstretched hands
dangling in the river
of the Milky Way.

Still, cold snow
darkness shivering
breath of awe
hanging visible on air.

When the city bustle,
political-hustle
of humanity's madness
grows soul-wearyingly
overwhelming
to me

I close my eyes
and find my way
up north,
within reach
of those stars.

In the Kingdom

Skylandia began
as an invention
of my grandfather,
a set of stories
set in a mythic realm
where brothers, sisters, cousins
could be queens, princesses,
princes (or royal acrobats)
without murdering
each other
for power.

Where wyverns evaded massacre
entranced by the Mango-Tango
danced by the hoof steps
of the Mango Moose
and Spotted Lion.

We named our farm
Skylandia
and added
more mythos
to the saga.

Skylandia would be
a place where
children could grow up whole
plants flourished without chemicals
and all the bills got paid.

Two out of three
in the harsh reality
of this world
is a good batting average
for the mythic.

Roadside Farm Stands

Years ago, they sat
strung like roadside shrines
along the northern tip
of Route One,
farm stands boasting
their wares in French:

Eshallots
Framboise
Haricot Verts
Pomme de Terre

Narrow structures
the size of outhouses
painted white
with shingled roofs
green trim
or occasionally
red.

Sturdy little shrines,
these Acadian farm stands.

I'll drive that road,
come summer,
pilgrimage to each one,
see the works of worship
of industrious gardeners
and considerate potato farmers
who put out ten pound bags

for local m'tantes and m'oncles
before shipping truckloads south
to the factories.

I wonder how many farm stands
are still standing,
still full,
still using the
old honor till
still displaying their signs
in French.

I wonder.

Farmhouse

Hundred years old,
this farmhouse is,
and not one
growing-up day
did I think
of its venerable age,
the walls brimming over
with so much
rambunctious now,
antiquity couldn't
cram a word in edgewise.

Rafters in the eaves
bear the hand-carved name,
Hector Dumais,
father of eighty-year old Valier,
who sold us the farmhouse
in the growing dusk
of his life
and let our family
spill fresh wildness
on the floors.

A hundred years heap up fast
between the turn of last century
and the dawn of a millennium
now fifteen years in and counting.

The farmhouse echoes
past laughter

though now
the rooms
breathe quiet
and the house
creaks to itself
and sighs.
Eaves packed with history,
paint layered in secrets,
dust of the world
in the floorboards.

Walking the Edge

Not many thirty-three
year old women
remember walking
the edge of a beaver dam.

I do.

You get this
in your blood
and it shapes you.

The crisscross jumble
of water-stripped
sun bleached
arm bone wide
branches,
grasses growing
out of the packed mud top,
still water pooling, black
tiny trickles seeping out,
bottom of the dam
run with weeds.

This is an old structure
smooth on the top
practically flattened
down into a path.

For who?
My siblings?

The beavers?
The deer?

Only today
do I realize
the rarity
of this experience.

Only today
do I realize
its worth.

Walking on the edge
of a beaver dam.

Down On My Knees In Devotion

Down on my knees
in the goodness of this earth,
her fertility etched
in the lines of my skin.

Throb of solidity,
heat of soil,
I am a child
of this mother.

I'll worship her
straight from the ground,
pull up a carrot,
swivel my fingers
around orange,
brush off dirt,
munch mineral grit,
and let the sweetness explode
on the tongue.

Fresh as ten seconds of time.

Crouched in blueberries,
gathering dark pearls,
rolling them in palm.
One hour for a jar.
That is devotion,
the feel of the crown
in your mouth.

Sung praises
to rainbows
in four languages,
one tongue,
exaltation,
rejoicing in wonder.

Child of my mother,
daughter of this earth,
no shame in worshiping her.

No mysterious connection,
divine plain as day,
no metaphorical communion,
bread is literal loaves,
grown from grain,
gift from the earth,
carrier of our bodies.

A farm girl,
I grew up
down on my knees
in devotion.

Bouquets of Mother

My mother,
Kathryn,
a name standing
tall on two feet
strong like the black coffee
she drank.

My mother
drove tractors
and wrangled
five children
through chores
last minute homework
breakfast cereal
dish duty
and onto the school bus
before the sun split
a crack in the sky.

My mother
cut armloads of bouquets
from the immense
bursting forth of the yard
day lilies, bold orange
Queen Anne's Lace, ocean spray white
irises, lavender
royal tongues of vetch
humble buttercups
primroses walloping the house
with perfume.

My mother
stretched into a tree
with her length of limbs, reaching
for the top shelf of vases,
lined up sensuous, round
glass women curved with grace.

My mother
must have heard
turn-of-the-century
ghost voices of women
on strike from factories
and endless days of labor,
singing for bread
for their children
and roses
for their souls.

My mother
knew working
from dawn long into the dark,
moving from housework
to fieldwork to homework
to exhaustion
and on the table
like a promise
stood the armloads
of flowers
held in the curved arms
of a vase.

Selling Poetry, Not the Farm

Of all the darn crazy schemes
cooked up on the farm
to pay down the taxes,
pay up the mortgage,
fix tractors,
keep the heat on,
and our heads above water. . .
this takes the three story cake.

Sell poetry, not the farm?

Good goddess.
Let me catch moonbeams
in silver nets
and sell them on Fifth Avenue
to high couture fashionistas
from France.

I don't know how
such a practical
Maine family
came to this.
Six generations
of hard working,
stoic,
pragmatic,
taciturn,
working-class people,
bricklayers,
fishermen,

ditch diggers,
horse team drivers,
and now,
this great-great granddaughter
writing poetry.

Must be my father's side,
scientists,
astronomers,
theater troupe managers,
writers stretching
back to Emerson,
and some Romanian grandmother,
thrown into the mix . . .

Yes, the nonsense of poetry
comes out of that side.
Though my mother's
Irish Catholics relatives
are to blame
for the storytelling.

Come to think,
my mother got the short stick
of the hair brained ideas.
We didn't try half of her
light bulb flash notions,
which were no more
Quixotic than my father's.

Like the time we raised pigs
that weren't pets,

named Porker and Bacon,
who grew into
700, 800lb
behemoths.
My father fell
head over pig heels
in LOVE
with those
smart-assed,
intelligent-eyed
oinkers,
that, needless to say,
never crossed
our dinner plates
on that long table
in the kitchen of the farmhouse.

If it had been left to my father,
we'd be citizens of Greenland
(no joke)
and since my mother
dug in her heels
with more grace,
determination,
and strength,
than the sow of our piglets
(who leapt a six foot fence
with her thousand pound heft)
we grew up
on the border of compromise,
as far north as you can get
and still claim citizenship

to the continental United States,
just spitting distance
from the river boundary
of Canada,
cooking up
crazy schemes
to keep the land,
raise kids,
and stay sane
all at the same time.

Quixotic doesn't cover
the half of it.

But here we are,
twenty sunchoke and strawberry
bare foot hardworking
summers later,
five kids full grown
still paying down bills
with madcap schemes
like peddling poetry
instead of the farm.

Raspberry Queen

Seven dollars a pint!
Half pint, I'm corrected,
and the pressure release valve
of my steam engine
whistle-clatter-hisses
but by some grace of God
does not break.

Not today,
I say calmly,
turning aside,
head held regally high.

The vendor at the farmers' market
just insulted
the Raspberry Queen
of Skylandia Farm
who has personally picked
with her own two fingers
more rosy jewels
than most people
see in their lifetime.

Seven dollars a half pint?!

I swivel back,
just in case
I heard that wrong
but no,
some boutique clothed

woman is paying the price,
tasting a sample,
enraptured.

Gag me.

At the height of the season,
the sight of a raspberry
turned my stomach,
tongue blistered from berry acid
taint of copper mold lingering
the smell of gray mold spores
caught in my nostrils
and the crunch of seeds
stuck in my teeth.

Sure, those raspberries
look season-start
mouthwateringly good,
but I will not drop
seven dollars down
for a measly fifty berries
in a shallow plastic container.

I've got raspberry mounds
in my memory,
buckets, pounds in the freezer
shelves of jam, ruby,
berries coming out of my ears,
my eyes, my dreams,
little old ladies
U picking the vines,

while I chuck moldy globes
at my brothers,
leaving telltale bloodstains
of raspberry row battles
imprinted on the backs of their shirts.

In that overpriced
farmers' market
filled with women and money
I start laughing,
remembering it all.

Seven dollars a half pint?!
Good grief.
If we'd had the guts
to charge half as much,
I'd be boasting boutique clothes
and buying that half pint
right now.

The Other Maine

I'm from Maine, I say.
Oh! I *love* Maine,
comes the reply.

Well, I add shortly,
I'm from the other Maine.
(the one out-of-staters
don't go to on vacation)

The other ninety percent
of the state
that does not
border the ocean
involve antique shops
or quaint bed and breakfasts.

The other Maine
where property taxes
are always overdue
mortgage payments run late
and no one has
a goddamn Adirondack chair
perched on their porch
because they're
too busy to sit down
can't afford to buy one
and if you stop moving for a second
the bugs and bills
will eat you alive.

But, hey,
no hard feelings.
I *love* Maine, too.

I hope I to go on
vacation there, someday.

Efficiency

Craig's List post
catches my eye
a single word:

Efficiency.

Implying a home
for a body.

I lived there, once,
for five summers flat
my formative teenage years
bent in the raspberry canes
strawberry rows
potato fields
carrots, beets, onions
greenhouse tomatoes
lettuces, Swiss chard
cucumber, squash
and zucchini.

I knew efficiency
before womanhood.
I made a house in hard work
one gesture to the next
continuous, constant, fluid
economy of motion
thrift of gesture
streamlined
practical

proud.

Efficiency.

I've lived long
in that house.
Got paid by the hour
by the pound
by the quart, pint
and pallet,
paid to grow up
in that place.

Seems crazy to pay
rent for it now.

Mosquitos on Wall St.

Got mosquito buzz
swarming in my ears
despite acres of concrete
for miles.

Got blood-sucking
frenzy circling me,
long day's journey
south from
the north country.

Wall Street.

Huh.

Up in the dark
of the woods
mosquitos
suck dry
thousand pound moose
into crazy-eyed
mangy-haired
sacks of bones
running to the river
to drown their
misery
out of existence.

Takes a million
mosquitos

to run down a moose.

Yet here,
table's turned
and a few greedy suckers
wipe out the masses.

Open for Business

Maine . . .
open for business!

I choke on a pretzel
spew the crumbs
onto the dashboard.

They took down
The Way Life Should Be
sign at the southern
border of Maine
and put up the
calling card
of vampires.

Open for business . . .

Puts me in mind of prostitution.
Sign ought to have
two peaked mountains
spread wide open
with a Maine river
in the slit
of the vulva.

Open for business . . .
as a former Maniac,
I'm fuming at the
steering wheel
from Ogunquit to Portland,

envisioning clear cuts,
strip malls,
corporate-consumer invasions,
pipelines and fracking
tars sand oil trains,
chemical factories,
and hog farms
bigger than most
of our towns.

Open for business...
like a cheap whore,
paid in cash.

I finally pull over
and cry.

This state,
my state,
place of my birth,
pine forests that raised me,
lakes deep blue,
rivers running cold,
gangly moose,
shocking red maples,
sweet givers of syrup,
farmers and fishermen...

You are not
up for sale
to out-of-state
interests.

Fat checkbooks
have no right
to pinch your bottom,
squeeze your tits,
ogle you,
fuck you,
and leave.

Alive

Meeting for the first time
three thousand miles
as the crow flies
from where we grew up
a hop, skip, and short
car ride from one another
in Maine.

I look at her high cheekbones
guarded self-knowing
respect in her spine
head held high with
hard won dignity
long brown hair
straight as an arrow
and say,

"I thought you were dead."

Meaning her people, all of them
the whole of a nation.

I learned in school
that the natives
were gone
as if they
- poof! -
up and vanished,
leaving behind rivers of names,
counties called Penobscot,

Piscataquis, Kennebec,
Aroostook, Androscoggin,
and Sagadahoc.
Also, that those people *used to*
and *once did*
and now *no longer were*.

I think,
if we could have heard
each other's souls
there might have roared
a hurricane of sorrow
lashed with torrents of fury
and a bottomless chasm of loss.

I never asked her
what she felt
hearing my startled, blurted confession,
"I thought you were dead."
My courage failed me.

Yes, the courage
of this red headed lioness
who roars at my own
race's endless stream
of injustice
without a blink of concern
for safety
or what might happen
when the most powerful
people in the world
decide to squash me flat.

I could only
swallow hard
at the precipice of loss
and bite back hot tears of shame.

There is an intensity of mourning
that knows no name.

I am mourning lost time,
decades, centuries
lost cultures
missed friendships
generations of people
love affairs, laughter
wrestling matches
sly tricks
and the opportunities
for peoples to grow.
Mourning all that time
spent annihilating nations
then pretending the survivors
did not exist.

And I am choking
on the sudden resurrection
of ghosts that have been living
all this time.

"I thought you were dead,"
my mouth said, unbidden,
and wild hope dared
bloom in my heart.

There's no ignoring the past,
the reckoning stands before me.
We have to live
with what my people
did to her people
and still do today.
We've got to navigate
sharp rocks thrown
into the shores
of our pasts,
war barriers
intended to sink
the possibility of friend-ships
because the white flag of truce
was a lie
and white
became the color
of hatred.

If we could hear each other's souls
she might have heard mine say,
I love you.
And then flush mightily
from toe to red hair,
and stick my foot in my soul's mouth,
saying,
I love you. I'm sorry. Please forgive me.
ho'oponopono
a Hawaiian practice
appropriated
because my culture
has forfeited the sincerity

of our apologetic words
on account of our broken treaties.

What does one do
when cultural reckoning
takes the form of two women
total strangers
who lived and breathed
practically next door
to each other,
strangers,
one being told stories
about the non-existence
of the other?

What does one do
when Truth shows up
in all her glory
standing with brown
fathomless eyes,
real,
alive,
holding her head high
with hard won dignity?

I, for one,
wrapped my ignorance
into a bitter pill
called humility,
and began swallowing
it ten times a day.

Oh, my friend,
what a gift you are
in your
very being
alive.

North Slope Orchard

We planted a fruit tree orchard
on the northeast facing slope.

I can hear my ancestors groaning.

Doesn't everyone know
the south slope is best?
For saltbox farmhouses
orchards, and fields?

Apparently not.

I've seen six apples
from those trees
in two decades.

Six.

Somehow, this is
the exact story
the United States
faces as we
fumble our way
back home
to this Earth.

Born and Raised in California

One after the other,
I tumbled in love
with two men
born and raised in California.
Two soul mates' worth
of magic and timebending
lifetime flashbacks
and the sorts of synchronicities
not even Hollywood
would believe.

But neither one
understood this
fanatic devotion
to a place - Maine -
located in the boondocks
and backwaters
of nowhere.

Yes, I know,
California is the hands down
winner of the drop dead
gorgeous competition,
recipient of the
most stunning views award,
world-class destination
for all things bohemian,
shrouded in the myths
and mystique of a literary era
or two.

But some of us
(not from California)
have soft spots
in our hearts
for the ugly ducklings
of this world.
Yes, the real
ugly ducklings,
that won't grow up
to be swans
until Hell freezes over
and Maine's mosquitos
vanish in a flash of extinction.

No more words left,
no explanations
as to why
my soul turns north
dreaming of overcast skies,
bedraggled, half-logged woods
infested with blood-sucking insects.

California is
easy on the eyes,
beautiful, magical,
gloriously gorgeous,
but I'll confess,
some of us
get the hots
for lands of other adjectives:
rugged, uncouth

stubbornly independent
tenacious, indomitable
proud . . .

or some other
loin-quickening
quality like that.

Woods

Woods,
thick with scrub brush
hordes of black fly guards
boot soaking swampy spots
sodden, squelching hiking.

Woods,
wilds guarded
human access
relegated to the
limits of logging roads,
snowmobile and four-wheeler trails.

Woods,
impenetrable thickets
hard to imagine them
clear-cut stumps
exposed to the sky
full horizon open to eyes
scanning contours
of earth's acres, naked.

Woods,
resentful, perhaps,
remembering such stripping
death, resurgence,
resurrection,
still maturing,
growing,
healing.

Potato Barn

Temperature of a morgue
built long and narrow
like an oversized coffin
half-buried in the side
of a hill,
dark, shadowed
potassium smell
small mountains of spuds
cement floor to the metal roofline
stables of boards
separating varieties.
Here, Yukon Golds.
There, All Reds.
Beyond, the Russets,
and the smaller specialty lots
in barrels so old
they were built before me
wood smooth
with hand grease
from roughened unknown palms.
Quiet, dry dust,
damp rot spots
here and there.
Potato barn,
winter home
of the harvest
in this valley.

Onward!

Seems to me,
we planted
in a madcap frenzy
and hoped something
produced by fall.

Old Valier Dumais,
said plant by the moon,
but we planted
whatever, whenever
we could,
starting the first day
the impenetrable snowmelt mud
wouldn't swallow you
all the way to China,
and ending only when
the weeds threatened suffocation.

Onward!

Weeks of wrestling
chokes of grass
back from rows,
yanking wild mustard stalks
out by the wheelbarrow load
digging up thistle, thorns, and nettles
until we abandoned that struggle
to rescue wilting potatoes
from the invading beetle assault,
then . . . boom!

The farm stand, kitchen garden crops
came in.

Pick, haul, wash, bundle,
hear that August thunder
start to rumble,
beat potato tops,
grab a sweater,
all too soon,
autumn harvest starts.

Hard Rocks and Potatoes

I have picked potatoes
by tractor light
racing against darkness
and time
in the Earth's Grand Prix
around the distancing sun,
who always wins,
but sometimes
more of the harvest
makes it into the barn,
sometimes,
our frail human bodies
inch ahead in the race,
sometimes,
the light frost mornings
linger longer
than hard freeze nights
allowing us
to eke out
a meager existence.

Denial of darkness
keeps us picking,
grasping potatoes and rocks
that look alike to the eye
until cold-gloved fingers
feel the hard weight
of the difference
and stone-solid reality
in your palm.

Snow Carrots

Carrots, treasured,
plucked from the grip of winter
just as the first frost
licks them sweet.

Yanked out by
green leafy curls,
stiff-lipped in protest
of the cold.

We chop the tops,
red handled clippers
gripped in fingers
turned numb.

Clouds gather into swells
darkened by short days.
For years, if bitter,
I'd remind my mother
of the time we picked
carrots in that snow.

Desolation.

Days of
hands frozen
in an ache that haunts
me still.
Gray horizons,
flurries dropping

cheeks stinging
wind whip lashing
sky spitting insults
in our face.

Awake

Crack of dawn
odor of coffee
air hung motionless
in silent contemplation.

Autumn Crisp

Crisp is a bite
of tart, tree-picked apple
when autumn begins to nip,
when frost lines etch lace
on overnight windowpanes,
and ice clings to the edge
of the bucket.

Ground crunches underfoot
in aching morning air
then surrenders
its cold shoulder
to the sun.

The sky catches its breath
in the ribs of my chest
as days losing light
draw near.

Four O'clock Dark

Four o'clock darkness,
I kid you not!
Puts the dampers down
on the heart.

Awake,
but sleepwalking
like half-hibernated bears,
with the four o'clock dark
cloaking all.

The only way out
lies inward.

Into silence,
reflection,
introspection,
thought,
meals with five kids
not talking,
wrapped up inside
while the night
lasts forever,
four o'clock dark
unto dawn.

Breathless

Giddy from cold
so sharp
it could kill you
stabbing flesh
through six layers
of wool,
shocked silly
breathless, gasping,
can't breathe
this air
'til spring.

Dead of Winter

Dead of winter
when stillness
is the only verb
in sight.

Sky could crack
from cold,
brittle blue,
sharp edged
as iron.

Nights reminding
everyone of death
or the time
before conception,
black as forgetting.

Stars sucked out of sight
in the breathtaking
gasp of darkness.

Farm Marrow

Crunch these bones
on my funeral pyre
test the grit of my marrow
in the lab.
They'll confirm
that land
built my skeletal structure
and this body
holds farm marrow
in its bones.

North Country Mornings

On north country mornings,
you can slip between worlds
as easily as stepping out of bed,
rising half-groggy,
and walk out into the mist.

Light frost etching lace
on every gold meadow stalk,
fog hung off the ponds
hushed and reverent,
breath of earth
on the air.

Grasses standing frozen
alongside ochre
and umber
bronze wild plants
caught in bloom,
each seed head
separated in frost,
each short blade
spiked straight up
from the ground.

The old farm road,
leads only to mysteries,
the veil of morning
still lowered
to the edge
of the forest.

You hover,
bewitched,
as the light rises
fog lifts
and the land yawns
its way into day.

Baptism

I yearn for my urban friends
reared on the smell
of asphalt after rain
to stand soaked
in a meadow
sweet-scented
with summer
damp and delirious
with the odor
of wildflowers
heart throbbing
aroused
to their own
sensuality
awakened
in the baptism
of rain.

Agricultural Old

I am old
not primordial old,
agricultural old
bare feet in fresh dirt old
my blood remembers
way back
generations breathing
the heat of the ground
cool dampness of mornings
and the deep black
sigh of the night.

Good Earth

Golden grasses
swaying over
long swells
of hills.

A sweep of
breathless blue sky.
Perfect farm girl clouds,
fresh, fertile
clean, white laundry
sheets hung on the line.

North country days
never-ending,
time playing out
summer's spindle.

Wind blowing brightly,
lifting hair off hot necks,
sending mosquitos tumbling
bringing the scent
of good earth to the air.

Afternoon Patina

Bits of life
on sweaty skin
seeds of wild grasses
hair thin spines
of mustard weeds
fine dry silt
and dust
crushed mosquito limbs
sunburn peelings
spittle bug juice
weed sap, green and grinning
afternoon patina
of sun bronzed hard work
and the infernal buzz-whine
of a horsefly.

Days of Downpour

One month,
Niagara Falls
vacationed over Maine,
hovering above us
in a never-ending downpour
'til the rivers burst
into copper-brown deluges
churned thick with the body
of our hills.

Candlelight & Rain

Thicket of thunderstorms

Electricity outage
candles brought out
set on the table
howling darkness
whipping rain on the windows
thundering rooftops
drumrolling gutters

Candles soft flickering
a sense of quiet
throughout.

Compost Psalm

Sacred compost
altar perched
on the back pallet
of the three-sided bin
receiving the unwanted
with the perfect charity
of Catholic saints,
transforming refuse
with the grace
of bodhisattvas,
making alchemy black gold
riches of nations
small batch topsoil
nutrient-packed dirt,
pierced through and
aerated with earthworms.
Spade sinks gentle
into this wonder of miracles
fresh-turned,
time crafted
compost.

Thunderstorm Joy

On this thunderous afternoon,
relief breaks
the torment of gnats,
as the oppressive low-pressure sky
grows huffy, curses, and finally
loses her temper.

My siblings and I sprint
yelping, whooping with joy,
down from the fields,
through the rain
toward a couple hours
respite from work.

Slip, slap, sliding
on the mowed grass road,
squelching wet
blades lain flat
fat on their deep
green sides.

Soaked to the skin,
itch of bug bites
cold-shower soothed,
hot scalps eased,
hair plastered slick,
pants heavy with water,
hitched up in one hand,
bare feet pale as drowned worms.

We run, scattering
pooled up shallow puddles
as the rain pour sharpens
and dances.

Daybreak Poem

Waiting for sunrise
to write this poem down
fingers itching
to set ink scrawling
in the brushstrokes
of dawn-rustled
songbirds in flight.

The World Spoke Poetry

I was not a practical child.

How could I be,
when the world spoke poetry
to me?

Not logics or science
or plain ole English.
Metaphor, myth,
simile, subtlety,
mystery, hints,
associations, tongue twisters,
words turned upside down
and shaken,
revealing hidden
meanings
inside.

Tasks like changing motor oil
and putting tractors into gear
turned into fool's errands -
like speaking binary code to a mystic.

Metal, power tools,
construction,
machines -
oil to the water of me.

You could find me
daydreaming,

twisting sculptures
out of grass strands
weaving twigs
into what-nots
immersed in the poetry
of the world.

Skinny Onions

For the life of me,
I do not know
how those
skinny onions
grow.

Fragile tubes,
tiny,
sprouting,
awash
in hard cracked soil.

My perplexed scowl
at the onion field,
mirrors my mother's frown,
taking inventory
of inches of bare wrists
and scarecrow ankles,
sticking out
clothing cuffs,
as she wondered
if her bare foot
summer children
would be able to squeeze
into fall,
school clothes,
and shoes.

It's all miracles.

No one knows
how onions
and poor children
grow.

Transplant

She watched us
surreptitiously
to see if we were drooping
wilting, or thriving,
transplanted
from the small
mill town
to the sheer wilds
of this north woods
farm.

Five kids
each one slowly
settling shocked roots
into new soil
and then,
one miraculous day,
we blossomed!

Novelist Grown

Spin ten thousand stories
weeding spindly carrots
tell tales silently
during harvest
hands busy
mind free
a novelist
grown through
farm work.

Washed out all
my worst stories
in the secrecy
of manual labor,
buried crazy concoctions
in the deep brown soil
laid to rest fantasies
and wiped my hands clean

To get on
with the rest of my life,
and all the interesting stories
that came later.

Library Books

At the Lincoln Street Library
in the city of Chicago
a last remaining outpost of public space
where citizens can rest
and children come with parents
where a man finishes
a course of study
on his lunch break
his orange tape measure
pulled from his belt
placed on the table
alongside stacks of papers
and an army fatigue backpack.

I, itinerate writer,
hiding
from the battering
cold Chicago concrete
and clattering L train thunder
remembering the days
when my four scrawny siblings
poor rural white children
growing up in a rundown mill town
were hauled by my six foot tall mother
once a week
down the steep
Court Street hill
and back up
as she lugged
two canvas tote bags

loaded with books
four per child
twenty volumes or more.

My mother was strong
with determination
even on the uphill climb
to putting food on the table
and shoes on our feet.

I remember, one night,
nine o'clock
watching public television
when she won forty bucks
in the Maine State Lottery
and cried . . .
because only that miracle
put gloves on our fingers
that frostbitten year.

In the lean times,
there were no pizza nights
only endless variations on spaghetti
and occasionally
the cupboards reached
the stage of empty
only miracles can solve.
There were no treats
that cost cash
but every week
new books
were hauled up the hill

from the Auburn Public Library
containing exotic places
other worlds
beyond the endless
aching stretch
of making ends meet.

I think on those times
sitting in the Lincoln Street Library
a thousand miles
and twenty years
past the days
of a six foot tall mother's
struggle to get me
through a long string
of miracles
to today.

Family

Family,
is remembering
the time
your younger brother
stuck his adolescent head
through the rungs
of the second story staircase
and got stuck.
(on account of his ears)

Family,
is the argument
every time we retell
this donkey-arsed story
about which twin brother
or cousin
or neighborhood kid
was actually the idiot
who put his head through the rails.

Family,
is the way
we all worked together
to slip the butter-greased earlobes
back out to freedom,
and never told a soul
or school friend
who cried.

If it is Good . . .

My strong younger brothers,
twins,
giants of men,
six foot tall and counting,
red heads like blazing torches
against the sky,
have tattooed on their
muscled arms:

*If it is good,
and if it is right,
then it shall be.*

A quote,
apparently,
from our father,
another giant
who once towered
over his sons.

Oddly,
I have no memory
of the saying,
as if the mantra
of my Papa
slipped past
the ears of his eldest daughter.

What does it mean?

How can an oft repeated
saying skirt around
my line of hearing,
yet etch itself into
the skin and fiber
of my brothers?

Hot Tar Fiddler on the Roof

That summer
not quite come
when we climbed
onto the loose shingles
of the roof
of our childhood
and poured hot tar
and promises
to live, love, and let go
just as we always had done.

The younger brother
and sister started it
with a wild dare
to jiggle like Tevye
on the roof!
Pillows for bellies
and memorized lyrics
from back when
we were too young
to know about politics
of Israel & Palestine
and how the victims of genocide
can become genocidal.

Back then,
when we did not quite
realize America's existence
was steeped in the blood
of a continent's worth

of massacres.

Back then,
when ignorance
and innocence
blurred.

Older now,
a score of hot summers
under our belts,
we're up on the blistering
roof of survival
singing songs of
poor people everywhere,
if I were a rich man,
Ya ha deedle deedle . . .
even the lyrics
can't find words
to express luxuries
we can't even imagine.

As the day cools,
my twin sister
with the fiddle
saws sunset laments,
eyes getting teary
with life.

Memory Footage

For every grainy
black and white
reel of memory
I've got . . .

my younger sister
shoots back
some HD, widescreen
surround sound
instant replay
response.

No sweat, though.

'Cause Mama's
streaming live
Bollywood
in technicolor glory
onto the hundred foot
screen of the drive-in.

And, the two-bit critics
up in the peanut gallery
throw in their worthless opinions,
commenting on films
they've never watched.

Think I'll just
string up a white sheet
in the cool backyard

of my thoughts
and stream silent films
tonight.

Summer of Canning Tomatoes

"Market's saturated,"
my father'd sigh.

Even ridiculously low prices
couldn't move the crates
of the tomatoes piling up.

My urban-raised friends
mutter about famines,
food shortages,
climate catastrophes,
zombie apocalypses.

(The last of which,
I can do nothing about,
the others of which,
I'll throw in my two cents.)

This indignant farm girl
declares the earth fertile,
ample, producing more
than enough
even in times of drought,
pest, disease, or
out-of-whack weather.

And haven't you read,
that United Nations study,
demonstrating that
ninety percent of famines

all the way back to Moses
are the fault
of human greed
and market manipulations?

And let me tell you
about the summer,
when I turned
fifteen years old,
tee-shirt sleeves
rolled to the shoulders,
cut off shorts,
bug bites and vanity
comingling . . .
that summer when,
along with my sisters,
mother, aunt, grandmother,
canned greenhouses worth
of tomatoes,
until our eyebrows
singed on steam
and our faces out-glowed
the reddest of the shiny
round orbs.

My brothers picked,
along with my father.
I suppose.
It's all blurred rows of jars
pops of pressure,
an occasional shattering sound.

My devotion
to this Earth,
my absolute faith,
was initiated that summer
by the overwhelming
abundance of tomatoes.

Flatbed Truck

Blue peeling paint
or was it red?
equally rusty in either case
with a smoker's cough engine
and a wooden flatbed,
one corner rotted out in the rain.

Five foot nothing,
getting younger every year
my grandmother, DeLores
(an odd spelling,
for an odd name,
for a Midwest daughter
of Swedes)
surprised the living daylights
out of two sons,
daughters-in-law,
assorted grandchildren,
and a handful of barn cats,
by announcing one afternoon
that she'd always wanted to be a trucker.

She's ninety this year,
that day took place in the vicinity
of her seventy-fifth birthday.
My know-it-all,
angle-elbowed,
teenage arrogance
had granma chalked up
as a housewife.

Three sons, a husband,
nice, modest house,
hosted annual holiday dinners
sent us checks on our birthdays
used matching tableware
even on weekdays
quiet, unassuming,
packed sandwiches
and Ziploc bags of potato chips
whenever she braved
the twelve-hour trip
up north.

And here she was
opening the Pandora's box
of a woman's truth,
slapping the pegs
and pigeonholes
out of her granddaughter's hands
announcing that she had
wanted to drive trucks.

Well, hot damn, I thought.
(though my mouth kept clean)

Her sons, a farmer and a woodsman,
exchanged long looks,
and silently opened the cab.

Why not?

None of her adolescent grandchildren

had crashed the flatbed truck,
the tractor, sit-down lawnmower,
snow blower, or the beat-up junker cars
that served as farm kid driving school.
Delores had a perfect driving record,
a valid license, and a heap more sense.
Besides, there was nothing
but fields to run into.

"Whoopee," she said.

And she rumbled up the hill,
hauling herself up on
the steering wheel to see.

I've got two sisters,
that now run a
cooperative distribution
company, delivering
product and produce
'cross the state.
They drive big trucks,
hold commercial licenses,
and share with me
this memory,
of our grandmother
driving that flatbed.

Growing Change

Thirteen years old
pulling weeds by hand
lobbing dirt clods
at my younger brothers.

That was the day
I became an activist,
though it took me two decades
and three thousand miles
to understand farm work
as social change.

Planting is an act of rebellion
to destruction as usual.
Picking potatoes changes systems
more than throwing rocks.

A cooperative of ten
miniscule northern Maine farms
dared to dream
of a future for families,
communities, peoples,
and this planet.

The story, very simply,
starts with my parents, sick,
of selling their souls to pay bills,
we left the big house in town
and headed for the hills,
the woods, the river, the ground.

I've been growing change
all my life,
sticking seeds in the earth,
getting smarter, sassier,
finding words for what once was
just plain old farming
and hard work.

(which my savvy activist friends
claim are prefigurative politics,
such a complicated word
for inventions of
desperate necessity,
like cooperatives to
get potatoes into markets,
and lobbying legislature for
non-draconian decisions,
and convincing philanthropic investors
that we need packing sheds not
opera houses,
and finding allies
hidden in pines,
tucked into coastal corners,
and down dirt roads
to nowhere.)

Gandhi, I learned,
two decades later,
coined a term for those
years of audacious dreams:
Constructive Program

another fancy word
for roughened palms
and self-respect
walking in the same
body of the people.

We were so shrouded
in blackflies and farm dust,
we couldn't see the movement
for the potato piles.

Spin cotton, said Gandhi,
liberate India.

Plant seeds, we said,
liberate our communities,
from greed and domination,
from being poor and isolated,
from depending on corporations
from Away,
(a place, in Maine-speech,
which implies anywhere beyond
the boundaries of the state).

Buy local food, we said,
grab your hard-earned dollars
back from far-away businesses
and hand them to your neighbors,
instead.

Picture my split face grin
and ear-to-ear smile,

when this farm girl laughs in joy
at all the changes that transpire
as we grow.

Hermit Crab Shell

Old childhood room
outgrown like a
hermit crab's shell
discarded and abandoned.

Long ago,
my soul burst out
the edges of those
pale blue walls
and crawled out
onto the roof,
leapt for the sky's embrace,
into the expanse
of clouds.

Ceiling of the nation,
north country sky,
light scraping boundaries
in that seamless
Robin's egg cup.

Drink up my soul,
pour the measure
of those years
into the draught
of all-knowing.

Swallow the past like a tonic.

No room can contain us, together.

Thirty-three

Thirty-three
womanhood
full-grown maturity
casting thoughts
through memory
sifting sieves
seines, warps, weaves
webs, wefts, nets
catching silver-backed
flashes of joy
gills of sorrow
loose threads
unraveled ends.

In the eaves
of the farmhouse
dusty boxes wait
baskets of photographs
bundles of baby clothes
old toys
hand sewn dolls
and the sounds
of our own ghosts
cast-off childhoods
left behind.

Been Gone Long

Been gone
long time,
still gone,
long distances
gone.

Yes, gone.

Yet, I cast my net,
that memory seine,
back to the lands
I carry.

It's like faith
this soil,
bonds of loyalty
and family.

I've got sisters
back there,
trees I grew up with,
now nieces and nephews,
and tenth generation
grandbabies of insects
I've been blood bonded
to since my childhood.

I've got that soil
inside me
that gritty mineral crunch.

I've got that
teeth aching
well water
somewhere
inside.

I've got the smell
of those pines
like a longing
inside me.

Blue sky
in my mind -
alright,
grey,
most days,
grey
in great banks
of thunderstorms,
rain clouds,
or snow.

I've been living
'round people
who look at me
crazy
when I tell them
the water just
falls from the sky.

And the crops grow,
the harvest comes,

and life keeps on churning.

All those years
and distances
long gone.

About the Author

Rivera Sun is the author of Billionaire Buddha, The Dandelion Insurrection and Steam Drills, Treadmills, and Shooting Stars, as well as nine plays, a study guide to nonviolent action, a book of poetry, and numerous articles. She has red hair, a twin sister, and a fondness for esoteric mystics. She went to Bennington College to study writing as a Harcourt Scholar and graduated with a degree in dance. She lives in an earthship house in New Mexico, where she grows tomatoes, bakes sourdough bread, and writes poetry, plays, and novels on the side. Rivera has been an aerial dancer, a bike messenger, and a gung-fu style tea server. Everything else about her - except her writing - is perfectly ordinary.

Rivera Sun also loves hearing from her readers.
Email: rivera@riverasun.com
Facebook: Rivera Sun
Twitter: @RiveraSunAuthor
Website: www.riverasun.com

www.ingramcontent.com/pod-product-compliance
Lightning Source LLC
LaVergne TN
LVHW041633070426
835507LV00008B/585

9780996639187